Because I Said So!!

100 AFFIRMATIONS FOR WOMEN WHO MEAN BUSINESS

BRITTNI BROWNE, MPS

Cover Illustrations by Xavier P. Hill

"She's made of Affirmations and Self-Love... You can't break a woman like that."

– Unknown

This book is dedicated to my strong, generous, beautiful, loving and praying mother, Marie.

Because of you, I know that the ability to achieve starts in the mind.

Because of you, I am.

Affirmation Categories

Self-Love
Affirmations #1-20

Gratitude
Affirmations #21-40

Career
Affirmations #41-60

Peace & Positivity
Affirmations #61-80

Environment
Affirmations #81-100

How To Use:

For Best Results

Spend Time With Yourself-
Yes, that means no phones, no social media, no distractions, just you.

Visualize Yourself In Possession-

By combining the repetition of affirmations with visualization, you are programming positive thought patterns into your subconscious mind.

Claim It!-

Repeat your affirmations confidently throughout the day. Remember to call those things that are not as though they were (Romans 4:17).

Self-Love.
Affirmations #1-20

Accommodated by self-care tips, quotes
and statements, with love.

Self-Love.

AFFIRMATION #001

Self-love is my divine right.

. . . .

SELF-LOVE ISN'T SELFISH. ON YOUR
SELF-LOVE JOURNEY, REMEMBER TO
PRIORITIZE YOURSELF, BE KIND TO
YOURSELF AND BE PATIENT WITH
YOURSELF.

@becauseisaidsobook

Self-Love.

AFFIRMATION #002

I am worthy of unconditional love.

....

WHEN LOVE IS UNCONDITIONAL, THERE ARE NO BOUNDS. UNCONDITIONAL LOVE IS MEANINGFUL AND EVERLASTING. LOVE YOURSELF UNCONDITIONALLY.

@becauseisaidsobook

Self-Love.

AFFIRMATION #003

I am well equipped with everything I need to walk in my purpose.

· · · · · · · · · · · · · · · · · · · ·

ALL THAT YOU ARE AND EVERYTHING
YOU HAVE IS ENOUGH.

Self-Love.

AFFIRMATION #004

I honor my mind and body and I take good care of myself.

....

MENTAL AND PHYSICAL HEALTH ARE
EQUALLY IMPORTANT. WHAT CHANGES
CAN YOU MAKE TODAY TO HONOR
YOUR MIND AND BODY?

@becauseisaidsobook

Self-Love.

AFFIRMATION #005

My relationship with myself is what's most important to me.

. . . .

SELF-CARE TIP: BE KIND TO YOURSELF.
TREAT YOURSELF HOW YOU WOULD
TREAT ANY OTHER RELATIONSHIP. GET
TO KNOW YOURSELF ON A DEEPER
LEVEL.

@becauseisaidsobook

Self-Love.

AFFIRMATION #006

I am in the process of becoming the best version of myself.

. . . .

YOU ARE YOUR OWN BIGGEST PROJECT. TRUST, ENJOY, AND FALL IN LOVE WITH THE PROCESS.

@becauseisaidsobook

Self-Love.

AFFIRMATION #007

I exude love and confidence, and it radiates from the inside, out.

. . . .

YOU GLOW DIFFERENTLY WHEN YOU ARE FULL OF LOVE AND CONFIDENT IN WHO YOU ARE.

@becauseisaidsobook

Self-Love.

AFFIRMATION #008

I honor my commitments to myself.

· · · · · · · · · · · · · · · · · · · ·

COMMIT TO YOUR DREAMS AND
GOALS. COMMIT TO ALL OF THE
THINGS THAT YOU WANT OUT OF
LIFE. COMMIT TO DOING THE WORK.
COMMIT TO YOUR PLAN OF ACTION.
COMMIT TO YOU.

@becauseisaidsobook

Self-Love.

AFFIRMATION #009

No struggle is greater than my strength.

· · · · · · · · · · · · · · · · · · · ·

JAMES 1:2-5: "CONSIDER IT PURE JOY, MY (BROTHERS AND) SISTERS, WHENEVER YOU FACE TRIALS OF MANY KINDS BECAUSE YOU KNOW THAT THE TESTING OF YOUR FAITH PRODUCES PERSEVERANCE. LET PERSEVERANCE FINISH ITS WORK SO THAT YOU MAY BE MATURE AND COMPLETE, NOT LACKING ANYTHING."

@becauseisaidsobook

Self-Love.

AFFIRMATION #010

I have the courage to say no to whatever makes me unhappy.

· · · · · · · · · · · · · · · · · · · ·

SELF-CARE TIP: SOMETIMES SAYING NO TO OTHERS MEANS SAYING YES TO YOURSELF. CHOOSE YOURSELF EVERY TIME.

@becauseisaidsobook

Self-Love.

AFFIRMATION #011

I release the need to prove myself to anyone.

. . . .

FIND OUT WHO YOU ARE AND OWN IT.
WHEN YOU LOVE YOURSELF, IT
DOESN'T MATTER WHAT ANYONE ELSE
THINKS ABOUT YOU.

@becauseisaidsobook

Self-Love.

AFFIRMATION #012

I have the courage to dream big, be bold and accomplish anything I put my mind to.

· · · · · · · · · · · · · · · · · · ·

SELF-CARE TIP: ALLOW YOUR IMAGINATION TO RUN WILD AND FREE.

@becauseisaidsobook

Self-Love.

AFFIRMATION #013

I am my own kind of beautiful. I love myself more and more, every day.

· · · · · · · · · · · · · · · · · · · ·

YOU ARE ONE OF ONE AND THAT IS THE MOST BEAUTIFUL THING ABOUT YOU.

@becauseisaidsobook

Self-Love.

AFFIRMATION #014

I trust myself to make the best decisions for me.

. . . .

SELF-CARE TIP: SEEK GUIDANCE
THROUGH PRAYER WHEN YOUR
SPIRIT FEELS INDECISIVE.

@becauseisaidsobook

Self-Love.

AFFIRMATION #015

I never give up on myself.

· · · · · · · · · · · · · · · · · · · ·

MARK 9:23: "'IF YOU CAN?'
JESUS SAID. 'EVERYTHING IS
POSSIBLE FOR ONE WHO
BELIEVES.'"

Self-Love.

AFFIRMATION #016

My health is important to me. I invest in it daily.

. . . .

SELF-CARE TIP: DAILY EXERCISE CAN HELP YOU PHYSICALLY AND MENTALLY. NOT ONLY CAN YOU GET IN SHAPE, BUT YOU CAN ALSO BOOST YOUR MOOD AND RELIEVE STRESS.

@becauseisaidsobook

AFFIRMATION #017

I live fearlessly in my truth.

. . . .

STAY TRUE TO YOUR AUTHENTIC
SELF. EMBRACE WHO YOU ARE AND
FALL IN LOVE WITH YOUR STORY.

Self-Love.

I know my self-worth. I am more than enough.

. . . .

A DAILY NOTE TO SELF.

@becauseisaidsobook

Self-Love.

AFFIRMATION #019

I have authority and dominion over every area of my life.

· · · · · · · · · · · · · · · · · · ·

GENESIS 1:26 "THEN GOD SAID, 'LET US MAKE MAN IN OUR IMAGE, AFTER OUR LIKENESS. AND LET THEM HAVE DOMINION OVER THE FISH OF THE SEA AND OVER THE BIRDS OF THE HEAVENS AND OVER THE LIVESTOCK AND OVER ALL THE EARTH AND OVER EVERY CREEPING THING THAT CREEPS ON THE EARTH.'"

@becauseisaidsobook

Self-Love.

AFFIRMATION #020

I am here for a divine purpose.

. . . .

SELF-CARE TIP: REFLECT ON HOW
FAR YOU HAVE COME. WRITE A
JOURNAL ENTRY TO YOUR
YOUNGER SELF.

@becauseisaidsobook

Gratitude.
Affirmations #21-40

Accommodated by Random Acts of
Kindness and Gratitude tips

Gratitude.

AFFIRMATION #021

I am grateful for the journey of self-discovery.

· · · · · · · · · · · · · · · · · · · ·

RANDOM ACT OF KINDNESS:
CALL YOUR GRANDPARENTS (OR AN
ELDER) TO EXPRESS YOUR
APPRECIATION FOR THEIR WISDOM.

@becauseisaidsobook

Gratitude.

AFFIRMATION #022

I am grateful for the blessings this day will bring.

. . . .

RANDOM ACT OF KINDNESS:
SPREAD SOME
ENCOURAGEMENT ONLINE.

@becauseisaidsobook

Gratitude.

I am grateful that my happiness is my responsibility.

. . . .

RANDOM ACT OF KINDNESS:
COMPLIMENT A STRANGER TODAY.

@becauseisaidsobook

Gratitude.

AFFIRMATION #024

I wake up at peace, grateful for life each day.

. . . .

RANDOM ACT OF KINDNESS:
DONATE OLD CLOTHES OR SUPPLIES
TO A LOCAL CHARITY.

@becauseisaidsobook

Gratitude.

AFFIRMATION #025

I am thankful for opportunities to create a life that I desire.

· · · · · · · · · · · · · · · · · · · ·

GRATITUDE TIP: WRITE DOWN FIFTY THINGS THAT YOU ARE GRATEFUL FOR.

@becauseisaidsobook

Gratitude.

AFFIRMATION #026

I invite gratitude into my heart.

· · · · · · · · · · · · · · · · · · · ·

GRATITUDE TIP: MEDITATE ON
WHAT YOU ARE GRATEFUL FOR

@becauseisaidsobook

Gratitude.

AFFIRMATION #027

I am grateful for God's guidance. I trust Him to lead me.

. . . .

RANDOM ACT OF KINDNESS:
PRAY FOR A STRANGER TODAY.

@becauseisaidsobook

Gratitude.

AFFIRMATION #028

I am grateful for the body that I have. Everyday it gets stronger.

....

GRATITUDE TIP: LIST TEN THINGS ABOUT YOUR BODY THAT YOU LOVE.

@becauseisaidsobook

Gratitude.

My gratitude attracts more to be grateful for.

. . . .

RANDOM ACT OF KINDNESS:
SURPRISE SOMEONE WITH COFFEE
(OR TEA).

@becauseisaidsobook

Gratitude.

AFFIRMATION #030

I am grateful for the lessons life teaches me. I learn something new each day.

. . . .

RANDOM ACT OF KINDNESS:
LEAVE A SMALL BUSINESS A 5-
STAR REVIEW.

@becauseisaidsobook

Gratitude.

AFFIRMATION #031

I am grateful
for the ability
to dream &
visualize.

....

RANDOM ACT OF KINDNESS:
SEND COLORING BOOKS TO
KIDS IN THE HOSPITAL.

@becauseisaidsobook

Gratitude.

AFFIRMATION #032

I am grateful for my free will to decide what's best for me.

· · · · · · · · · · · · · · · · · · ·

RANDOM ACT OF KINDNESS:
ASK SOMEONE HOW YOU CAN
ASSIST THEM WITH A PROJECT.

Gratitude.

AFFIRMATION #033

I am grateful for friends and family who make me laugh.

. . . .

GRATITUDE TIP: CALL A FRIEND OR FAMILY MEMBER TO THANK THEM FOR THE IMPACT THEY HAVE HAD ON YOUR LIFE.

@becauseisaidsobook

Gratitude.

AFFIRMATION #034

I no longer complain. I choose to be grateful for this moment right now.

· · · · · · · · · · · · · · · · · · · ·

GRATITUDE TIP: WRITE DOWN THE NEGATIVE THOUGHTS THAT YOU HAVE AND THE POSITIVE THOUGHTS YOU WILL REPLACE THEM WITH MOVING FORWARD.

@becauseisaidsobook

Gratitude.

AFFIRMATION #035

I am grateful for the cells and organs in my body. I am well.

. . . .

GRATITUDE TIP: THANK A HEALTH CARE PROFESSIONAL FOR THEIR SERVICE.

@becauseisaidsobook

Gratitude.

AFFIRMATION #036

I woke up today. I feel blessed and thankful.

. . . .

GRATITUDE TIP: TAKE TIME TO APPRECIATE THE SUNRISE AND SUNSET TODAY.

@becauseisaidsobook

Gratitude.

AFFIRMATION #037

I am always
finding new
things to
appreciate in
life.

· ·

RANDOM ACT OF KINDNESS:
BRING IN MORNING TREATS FOR
YOUR COWORKERS.

@becauseisaidsobook

Gratitude.

AFFIRMATION #038

I am grateful for a roof over my head and food in my stomach.

....

GRATITUDE TIP: VOLUNTEER FOR (OR DONATE TO) A NONPROFIT ORGANIZATION THAT FEEDS OR PROVIDES SHELTER FOR THOSE IN NEED.

@becauseisaidsobook

Gratitude.

AFFIRMATION #039

I am grateful to be in a position to provide for others.

· · · · · · · · · · · · · · · · · · ·

RANDOM ACT OF KINDNESS:
DO A FAVOR FOR SOMEONE
WITHOUT EXPECTING ANYTHING IN
RETURN.

@becauseisaidsobook

Gratitude.

AFFIRMATION #040

Good things come to me because I am grateful.

. . . .

GRATITUDE TIP: PARTICIPATE IN
A FUNDRAISER THROUGH A
LOCAL NON-PROFIT.

@becauseisaidsobook

Career.
Affirmations #41-60

Accommodated by Quotes from profound women who inspire us to be our best selves.

Career.

AFFIRMATION #041

I manifest everything that I desire.

. . . .

"INSTEAD OF LOOKING IN THE PAST, I PUT
MYSELF TWENTY YEARS AHEAD AND TRY
TO LOOK AT WHAT I NEED TO DO NOW, IN
ORDER TO GET THERE THEN."

- DIANA ROSS
SINGER, ACTRESS AND RECORD PRODUCER

@becauseisaidsobook

Career.

AFFIRMATION #042

I am prepared to tackle every task on my to-do list today.

. . . .

"DREAMS DO NOT COME TRUE JUST
BECAUSE YOU DREAM THEM. IT'S HARD
WORK THAT MAKES THINGS HAPPEN. IT'S
HARD WORK THAT CREATES CHANGE."

-SHONDA RHIMES
AWARD WINNING TELEVISION PRODUCER,
SCREENWRITER AND AUTHOR

@becauseisaidsobook

Career.

AFFIRMATION #043

I am committed to my professional and financial goals.

....

"BELIEVE IN YOURSELF, LEARN, AND NEVER STOP WANTING TO BUILD A BETTER WORLD."

-MARY MCLOUD BETHUNE
EDUCATOR, PHILANTHROPIST, CIVIL RIGHTS ACTIVIST AND FOUNDER OF BARBER SCOTIA COLLEGE

Career.

AFFIRMATION #044

I am a leader with great character and high integrity.

. . . .

"THE SUCCESS OF EVERY WOMAN SHOULD BE THE INSPIRATION TO ANOTHER."

-SERENA WILLIAMS
WORLD CLASS TENNIS PLAYER AND BUISNESSWOMAN

@becauseisaidsobook

Career.

AFFIRMATION #045

I view challenges as opportunities to grow.

. . . .

"I DON'T HARP ON THE NEGATIVE,
BECAUSE IF YOU DO, THEN THERE IS
NO PROGRESSION. YOU GOT TO
ALWAYS LOOK ON THE BRIGHT SIDE
OF THINGS."

-TARAJI P. HENSON
AWARD WINNING ACTRESS, AUTHOR AND
BUSINESSWOMAN

@becauseisaidsobook

Career.

I am dedicated to enhancing my craft.

. . . .

"I'D RATHER REGRET THE RISKS THAT DIDN'T WORK OUT THAN THE CHANCES I DIDN'T TAKE AT ALL."

-SIMONE BILES
WORLD-CLASS GYMNAST

@becauseisaidsobook

Career.

AFFIRMATION #047

I am confident, capable, and consistent. I can do anything I put my mind to.

. . . .

"YOU ARE ON THE EVE OF COMPLETE
VICTORY. YOU CAN'T GO WRONG.
THE WORLD IS BEHIND YOU."

-JOSEPHINE BAKER
CIVIL RIGHTS ACTIVIST AND ENTERTAINER

@becauseisaidsobook

Career.

I am a valuable asset to any organization that I associate myself with.

. . . .

"HOW CAN ANY DENY THEMSELVES THE PLEASURE OF MY COMPANY? IT'S BEYOND ME."

-ZORA NEALE HURSTON
WORLD CLASS AUTHOR AND FILM MAKER

@becauseisaidsobook

Career.

AFFIRMATION #049

I will not place limitations on myself, or my ability to get things done.

....

"IF YOU'RE DOING SOMETHING OUTSIDE OF DOMINANT CULTURE, THERE'S NO EASY PLACE FOR YOU. YOU WILL HAVE TO DO IT YOURSELF."

-AVA DUVERNAY
WORLD CLASS FILMMAKER

@becauseisaidsobook

Career.

AFFIRMATION #050

I operate in excellence. I always give 100% effort in all that I do.

. . . .

"EXCELLENCE IS THE MOST POWERFUL
ANSWER YOU CAN GIVE THE DOUBTERS
AND HATERS."

-MICHELLE OBAMA
FORMER FIRST LADY OF THE UNITED STATES,
AUTHOR, AND ATTORNEY

@becauseisaidsobook

Career.

AFFIRMATION #051

I am an innovator. If what I want does not exist, I create it.

· · · · · · · · · · · · · · · · · · ·

"I HAD TO MAKE MY OWN LIVING AND MY OWN OPPORTUNITY. DON'T SIT DOWN AND WAIT FOR OPPORTUNITIES TO COME. GET UP AND MAKE THEM."

– MADAM C.J. WALKER
ENTREPRENEUR, PHILANTHROPIST, AND ACTIVIST

Career.

AFFIRMATION #052

I welcome financial abundance into my life.

······················

"LET GO AND OPEN YOUR HEART TO THE POSSIBILITY THAT THERE IS SOMETHING GREAT WAITING FOR YOU."

-IYANLA VANZANT
INSPIRATIONAL SPEAKER, AUTHOR AND LIFE COACH

@becauseisaidsobook

Career.

I always do whatever it takes to accomplish my goals.

. . . .

"THERE HAVE BEEN SO MANY PEOPLE WHO HAVE SAID TO ME 'YOU CAN'T DO THAT,' BUT I HAD AN INNATE BELIEF THAT THEY WERE WRONG. BE UNWAVERING AND RELENTLESS IN YOUR APPROACH."

-HALLE BERRY
AWARD WINNING ACTRESS

@becauseisaidsobook

Career.

I overcome every challenge that comes my way.

· · · · · · · · · · · · · · · · · · · ·

"I THRIVE ON OBSTACLES. IF I'M TOLD IT
CAN'T BE DONE, THEN I PUSH HARDER."

-ISSA RAE
AWARD-WINNING ACTRESS, WRITER, AND
PRODUCER

@becauseisaidsobook

Career.

AFFIRMATION #055

My work makes a difference in the world.

. . . .

"SUCCESS ISN'T ABOUT HOW MUCH
MONEY YOU MAKE. IT'S ABOUT THE
DIFFERENCE YOU MAKE IN PEOPLE'S
LIVES."

-MICHELLE OBAMA
FORMER FIRST LADY OF THE UNITED STATES,
AUTHOR AND ATTORNEY

@becauseisaidsobook

Career.

AFFIRMATION #056

My team and support system encourages me to stay committed to my goals.

· · · · · · · · · · · · · · · · · · ·

"SURROUND YOURSELF ONLY WITH PEOPLE WHO ARE GOING TO TAKE YOU HIGHER."

-OPRAH WINFREY
ENTREPRENEUR, HOST, AUTHOR, AND PHILANTHROPIST

@becauseisaidsobook

Career.

AFFIRMATION #057

I am worth the investment.

....

"I GOT MY START BY GIVING MYSELF A START."

-MADAM C.J. WALKER
ENTREPRENEUR, PHILANTHROPIST AND ACTIVIST

@becauseisaidsobook

Career.

AFFIRMATION #058

I am doing the best that I can. I am proud of how far I've come.

. . . .

"DO THE BEST THAT YOU CAN
UNTIL YOU KNOW BETTER. THEN
WHEN YOU KNOW BETTER, DO
BETTER."

-MAYA ANGELOU
WORLD RENOWNED POET AND ACTIVIST

@becauseisaidsobook

Career.

I am focused on building my empire!

. . . .

"I HAVE STANDARDS I DON'T PLAN ON LOWERING FOR ANYBODY, INCLUDING MYSELF."

– ZENDAYA
AWARD WINNING ACTRESS

@becauseisaidsobook

Career.

AFFIRMATION #060

I always stay true to myself and my core values.

. . . .

"I CAME INTO THIS COMPETITION WITH MY NATURAL HAIR AS A SYMBOL OF MY FIRM BELIEF IN BEING YOURSELF."

-ZOZIBINI TUNZI
MISS UNIVERSE 2019

@becauseisaidsobook

Peace & Positivity

Affirmations #61-80

Accommodated by meditation exercises, scriptures and tips for ultimate peace.

AFFIRMATION #061

Today I am giving myself permission to start over & start fresh.

. . . .

IT'S <u>NEVER</u> TOO LATE FOR A NEW BEGINNING!

@becauseisaidsobook

AFFIRMATION #062

I choose to refocus my energy on what brings me peace.

· · · · · · · · · · · · · · · · · · · ·

INNER-PEACE IS A CHOICE.

AFFIRMATION #063

I am powerful enough to overcome negativity and anxiety.

. . . .

CHOOSE A POSITIVE PERSPECTIVE. FIND THE OPTIMISTIC VIEWPOINT IN NEGATIVE SITUATIONS.

AFFIRMATION #064

I attract new opportunities, everyday.

· ·

BE OPEN-MINDED AND OPTIMISTIC
ABOUT THE NEW EXPERIENCES
THAT ARE COMING YOUR WAY.

AFFIRMATION #065

I am eliminating what does not help me evolve.

. . . .

IF IT'S NOT HELPING YOU GROW
SPIRITUALLY, PHYSICALLY,
EMOTIONALLY, MENTALLY, OR
FINANCIALLY... LET IT GO.

AFFIRMATION #066

I am worthy of peace, love, and happiness.

....

ADD VALUE AND POSITIVITY TO
SOMEONE'S LIFE TODAY. WHAT
YOU PUT OUT INTO THE WORLD
RETURNS IN ABUNDANCE.

@becauseisaidsobook

AFFIRMATION #067

I release any stress or worry that may cloud my mind.

. . . .

TAKE A DEEP BREATH IN. AS YOU
EXHALE, REPEAT THE AFFIRMATION
ABOVE. REPEAT AS MANY TIMES AS
NECESSARY.

AFFIRMATION #068

I choose to move with a positive and abundant mindset.

· ·

PHILIPPIANS 4:8 "FINALLY, (BROTHERS AND) SISTERS, WHATEVER IS TRUE, WHATEVER IS NOBLE, WHATEVER IS RIGHT, WHATEVER IS PURE, WHATEVER IS LOVELY, WHATEVER IS ADMIRABLE— IF ANYTHING IS EXCELLENT OR PRAISEWORTHY— THINK ABOUT SUCH THINGS."

@becauseisaidsobook

AFFIRMATION #069

Today will be filled with positive vibrations only.

. . . .

WHEN YOU VIBRATE HIGH, YOU SPREAD
FEELINGS OF PEACE, LOVE, KINDNESS
AND COMPASSION.

@becauseisaidsobook

AFFIRMATION #070

I release any judgmental thoughts or comparisons from my mind.

· · · · · · · · · · · · · · · · · · ·

YOU ARE ONE OF ONE. PLEASE DO NOT COMPARE YOURSELF TO YOUR COWORKERS, NEIGHBORS, OR STRANGERS ON THE INTERNET.

@becauseisaidsobook

AFFIRMATION #071

I grant myself peace of mind. I feel calm and balanced.

· · · · · · · · · · · · · · · · · · ·

LIVE IN THE MOMENT TODAY. TAKE A FEW MINUTES TO FOCUS ON WHAT'S GOING ON AROUND YOU. FREE YOUR MIND, OPEN YOUR ARMS WIDE, AND REPEAT TODAY'S AFFIRMATION OUT LOUD.

AFFIRMATION #072

I will not let anyone take me to a place that I've leveled up from.

• • • • • • • • • • • • • • • • • • • •

1 CORINTHIANS 13:13 "AND NOW THESE THREE REMAIN- FAITH, HOPE, AND LOVE. BUT THE GREATEST OF THESE IS LOVE."

@becauseisaidsobook

AFFIRMATION #073

I always choose faith over fear.

. . . .

ISAIAH 41:10: "SO DO NOT FEAR, FOR I AM WITH YOU; DO NOT BE DISMAYED, FOR I AM YOUR GOD. I WILL STRENGTHEN YOU AND HELP YOU; I WILL UPHOLD YOU WITH MY RIGHTEOUS RIGHT HAND."

AFFIRMATION #074

What's meant to be, will be & what's for me will never pass me by.

. . . .

KNOW THAT EVERYTHING IS
WORKING IN YOUR FAVOR, FOR THE
GREATER GOOD OF YOUR LIFE.

@becauseisaidsobook

AFFIRMATION #075

I release all toxic energy and negativity that blocks my soul from shining.

. . . .

MATTHEW 5:14-16 "YOU ARE THE LIGHT OF THE WORLD. A TOWN BUILT ON A HILL CANNOT BE HIDDEN. NEITHER DO PEOPLE LIGHT A LAMP AND PUT IT UNDER A BOWL. INSTEAD, THEY PUT IT ON ITS STAND, AND IT GIVES LIGHT TO EVERYONE IN THE HOUSE. IN THE SAME WAY, LET YOUR LIGHT SHINE BEFORE OTHERS, THAT THEY MAY SEE YOUR GOOD DEEDS AND GLORIFY YOUR FATHER IN HEAVEN."

@becauseisaidsobook

AFFIRMATION #076

I will experience new beginnings in ways that I've never imagined.

· · · · · · · · · · · · · · · · · · · ·

BIG THINGS ARE ON THE HORIZON.
STEP INTO YOUR GREATNESS.

Peace + Positivity

AFFIRMATION #077

Everything will work out in my favor today.

· · · · · · · · · · · · · · · · · · · ·

MOVE THROUGHOUT THE DAY WITH
CONFIDENCE. GOD HAS ALREADY
WORKED EVERYTHING OUT FOR YOU.

@becauseisaidsobook

AFFIRMATION #078

I let go of any stress and anxiety weighing heavy on me.

· · · · · · · · · · · · · · · · · · · ·

1 PETER 5:7: CAST ALL YOUR ANXIETY ON HIM BECAUSE HE CARES FOR YOU.

@becauseisaidsobook

AFFIRMATION #079

Today I am claiming peace within. I trust that I am exactly where I need to be.

· · · · · · · · · · · · · · · · · · · ·

REST AND RELAX IN GOD'S PRESENCE. LET GO OF ANY ANXIOUS THOUGHTS. LESS RUSHING, AND MORE PRAYING.

@becauseisaidsobook

AFFIRMATION #080

I am developing positive thought patterns. My positive thoughts always lead to positive results.

. . . .

MEDITATION EXERCISE: SIT STILL, BLOCK OUT THE NOISE AND TAKE DEEP BREATHS. AS YOU CALM YOUR MIND AND BODY, MEDITATE ON THE THINGS THAT BRING YOU JOY AND INSPIRE YOU DAILY.

Environment.
Affirmations #81-100

Accommodated by practical tips and
questions to improve your environment.

Environment

AFFIRMATION #081

I am aware of my inner nature. I live in it daily.

. . . .

AWAKEN YOUR CONNECTION TO NATURE. QUIET YOUR MIND AND ALLOW NATURE TO IGNITE YOUR SENSES AND SOOTHE YOUR SOUL.

Environment

I only surround myself with people who bring out the best in me.

. . . .

TAKE AN INVENTORY OF THE
PEOPLE AROUND YOU.

@becauseisaidsobook

Environment

AFFIRMATION #083

I open my
heart to
people, places,
and things that
make me feel
like magic.

....

EXPLORE A NEW HOBBY TODAY.

@becauseisaidsobook

Environment

I am connected to my core essence and the wisdom that surrounds me.

. . . .

TAKE SOME TIME TO CHECK IN WITH YOURSELF. ARE YOU LEARNING SOMETHING NEW EVERY DAY?

@becauseisaidsobook

Environment

My awareness is constantly expanding and inspiring my creativity.

· · · · · · · · · · · · · · · · · · · ·

LOOK AT ALL THE THINGS AROUND YOU THAT WERE THOUGHT OF BY ANOTHER HUMAN, THAT CAME TO LIFE. LET THAT INSPIRE YOU TO LIVE IN YOUR GREATNESS!

@becauseisaidsobook

Environment

AFFIRMATION #086

I surround myself with those who accept & appreciate all of me.

· ·

ACKNOWLEDGE YOUR SUPPORT SYSTEM. SEND A CARD OR TEXT, OR CALL THEM, SIMPLY TO SAY THANK YOU!

Environment

I embrace learning from the things that surround me daily.

. . . .

SEEK TO LEARN SOMETHING NEW,
EVERY DAY.

@becauseisaidsobook

Environment

I live in an environment that supports my overall well-being.

· · · · · · · · · · · · · · · · · · · ·

PRIORITIZE YOUR ATMOSPHERE TODAY. MAKE THE ADJUSTMENTS NECESSARY TO ALIGN YOUR SURROUNDINGS WITH YOUR DESIRED LIFESTYLE.

@becauseisaidsobook

Environment

AFFIRMATION #089

I shine bright in every room that I walk in.

·····················

TRANSFER YOUR POSITIVE ENERGY
TO SOMEONE WHO MAY NOT BE
HAVING A GOOD DAY.

@becauseisaidsobook

Environment

AFFIRMATION #090

I am in vibration with the earth. I am in harmony with nature.

. . . .

RECONNECT WITH YOUR PLACE IN THE NATURAL WORLD.

@becauseisaidsobook

Environment

I am flexible with the changes happening in my life.

· · · · · · · · · · · · · · · · · · · ·

CHANGES, WHETHER THEY SEEM GOOD OR BAD, WILL ALWAYS TEACH YOU SOMETHING NEW AND PREPARE YOU FOR THE FUTURE.

@becauseisaidsobook

Environment

AFFIRMATION #092

I attract people who vibrate at the same frequency as me.

· · · · · · · · · · · · · · · · · · ·

BE INTENTIONAL ABOUT KEEPING
YOUR VIBRATIONS HIGH.

@becauseisaidsobook

Environment

I choose to be around unlimited love and genuine people.

. . . .

SHARE YOUR ENERGY WITH PEOPLE
WHO MAKE YOU FEEL GOOD.

Environment

AFFIRMATION #094

I attract people
with kind
hearts and
pure intentions.

. . . .

MAKE SURE THE PEOPLE AROUND YOU
GOOD FOR YOUR MENTAL HEALTH.

Environment

AFFIRMATION #095

I associate myself with winners.

....

DO THE PEOPLE AROUND YOU
INSPIRE YOU TO BECOME A
BETTER VERSION OF YOURSELF?

Environment

AFFIRMATION #096

I am living life on my own terms and my surroundings reflect that.

· · · · · · · · · · · · · · · · · · ·

ARE YOU LIVING A LIFE THAT IS
MEANINGFUL AND FULFILLING
TO YOU?

@becauseisaidsobook

Environment

AFFIRMATION #097

I encourage the people around me to follow their dreams.

· · · · · · · · · · · · · · · · · · · ·

CALL AND CHECK ON A FELLOW
DREAMER, TODAY.

@becauseisaidsobook

Environment

AFFIRMATION #098

I have the power to create the life that I desire.

. . . .

2 TIMOTHY 1:7 "FOR THE SPIRIT GOD GAVE US DOES NOT MAKE US TIMID, BUT GIVES US POWER, LOVE, AND SELF-DISCIPLINE."

@becauseisaidsobook

Environment

I am focused on creating an inspiring space around me.

. . . .

YOUR SURROUNDINGS INFLUENCE
YOUR STATE OF MIND.

@becauseisaidsobook

Environment

AFFIRMATION #100

I feel good knowing that I am apart of something much bigger than myself.

. . . .

STRIVE TO LEAVE AN IMPRINT
ON THE WORLD.

@becauseisaidsobook

About The Author

As a former athlete and beauty pageant competitor, Brittni learned early in life that hard work, dedication, and persistence would contribute to achieving her goals. It was through competition, both as part of a team and an individual, that she developed her core values and characteristics, molding her to operate with high integrity, accountability, trust, patience, and a positive attitude. Now, having worked over one- thousand events, Brittni Browne is no stranger to the Sports and Entertainment industry. She has traveled coast-to-coast developing her industry portfolio as a behind-the-scenes operator, working for a variety of events and organizations, including the Charlotte Hornets, Kentucky Derby, US Open, PGA Championship, BNP Paribas Tournament, Wells Fargo Golf Championship, NBA All-Star Weekend, ACC Men's Basketball Tournament, and more.

Brittni received a Bachelor's degree in Marketing from North Carolina A&T State University, the largest HBCU in the world, and extended her education at Georgetown University, where she received her Master's degree in Sports Industry Management. In 2017, Brittni founded Browne Business Enterprises, LLC., the parent company to the three businesses in her current portfolio. The most recent addition to the family is BrowneDNA, inc., an event management and production company, where she and her staff develop and execute sports, entertainment, and corporate events and conferences.

Brittni relies on her faith to see her through. She credits organization, the use of affirmations, her ability to multi-task and develop strategic plans, and most importantly, her self-awareness to the success that she has had in the business. In 2019, Brittni challenged herself to be impactful outside of her industry, which lead her to author two books, "Because I Said So: 100 Affirmations For Women Who Mean Business" and "Set The Tone: A 10-Step Workbook To Establish Your Goals And Develop A Blueprint For Success." When Brittni is not producing an event, she devotes her time to mentoring and hosting free self-awareness workshops for college women, fulfilling her passion for helping individuals become the best version of themselves. Outside of conducting business, you can find her spending time with friends and family, exploring a new beach, or attending a sports or entertainment event for fun. You can follow her journey on Instagram @brittnibrowne, and connect with her on LinkedIn at www.linkedin.com/in/brittnibrowne.